Bible Contradictions?

John Taylor

johnebtaylor@yahoo.ca

ISBN 978-1-257-77134-9

Inspired by Holger and Joachim

Introduction

Many people have an idea in their minds that the Bible is 'full of contradictions'. In most cases this opinion was not formed as a result of either Bible reading or study, and so until the advent of online forums and blogs, asking them to show you one of those contradictions would generally end the discussion.

That situation has changed! Information of all kinds is readily available via the internet. In today's world it is only the work of a moment to access a list of Bible contradictions. Some items on these lists truly merit discussion, others are difficult to take seriously. However, when someone wants to demonstrate that there are difficulties in the Bible they will have something to back that assertion up!

The purpose of this book is to discuss some of these supposed contradictions from a Christian perspective. To investigate the validity of the claims being made, and to offer a response to them.

Contents

What is a Contradiction?

For the purpose of considering Bible contradictions the word, contradiction, must be taken in its broadest sense. In some cases the 'contradiction' involves two seemingly contrary statements about God, humanity, or some other topic. In other cases there are two accounts of what appears to be the same event, but each account includes significant differences. At other times the 'contradiction' could be more accurately termed a supposed inaccuracy, the Bible makes a claim which many people in the 21st century western world disagree with. In discussing Bible contradictions it will be important to determine in what sense the word is being used.

An example of seemingly 'Contrary Statements' can be found between Proverbs 4:7 and Ecclesiastes 1:18. Taking both passages at face value, Proverbs tells us of the importance of wisdom, and encourages people to acquire it. Ecclesiastes would seem to point the reader in a different direction, saying that wisdom leads to sorrow.

An example where we can notice 'Differing Accounts of a Single Event' can be found in the four Gospels, with the details of the first Easter Sunday morning. Matthew tells us that Mary Magdalene, and the other Mary went to Jesus' tomb. Mark mentions Mary Magdalene, Mary the mother of James, and Salome; but John only mentions Mary Magdalene.

Lastly some 'contradictions' fall under the category of supposedly inaccurate statements. This category would include accounts of miracles, as well as poetic or figurative descriptions of the physical world. Here it must be stressed that the term 'contradiction' is considerably stretched! A reader may not believe in the reliability of what he is reading because he or she does not believe in miracles, but that is not the same as a claim that the text itself is inconsistent.

Discussing Bible Contradictions

People raise the topic of contradictions or inconsistencies within the Bible from a wide range of motives. There are people who accept what the Bible has to say as true, but find that there are a number of its teachings that they struggle to understand. Others may not believe in Biblical teachings, but they are earnestly interested in discussing them anyway. And some want to make an attack on the beliefs of others, but have no real interest in dialogue.

Close to the beginning of any serious discussion you will need to understand where the other person is coming from. That is, do they actually want to talk, do they have real questions, to which they are seeking real answers; or are they merely trying to upset you. It may be helpful to ask whether the contradiction is something they have noticed through their own reading of the Bible, or something they found in a list someone else compiled. Ask them questions about the contradiction, have them explain it to you, find out if they fully agree with what they have read or harbour some reservations.

If a person has no interest in clarifying the contradiction then they are probably not truly interested in talking about it at all. You can offer to discuss the issue with them, but unless they too have some willingness to dialogue you may be wasting your time. Expressing your disagreement with their claim and offering to talk in more detail, (should they wish to at some future date) may be as far as things get.

Finally do not lose sight of the reason you are wanting to talk in the first place. That is, there is no point winning an argument, if in the process you destroy a relationship, or increase someone's determination to reject God. Be honest and clear in your communication, but don't be hostile or antagonistic. Don't forget that the person you are speaking to may have real, legitimate questions; and above all don't forget to be loving as you seek to communicate truth.

Reading with Understanding

When reading a portion of the Bible, or anything else, it is important to consider both the context, and the historical background of that writing. Taking a single sentence in isolation there might be a number of possible interpretations, each entirely plausible. Reading that sentence within a paragraph, or even several paragraphs will probably give you a clearer understanding of its intended meaning. Having some understanding of a statement's background setting will also help explain that statement. Knowing who made the comment in the first place, and to whom, will shed light on a command or comment that in isolation appears random or insignificant.

For example, take a command given towards the end of Second Timothy: *'When you come, bring the cloak that I left with Carpus at Troas...'*[1] This is neither a difficult nor a controversial passage, but it does illustrate the importance of historical background, and literary context.

Taking the passage on its own, in isolation, we do not know who is speaking to whom, nor why. A comment about clothing left in Troas (wherever that may be) seems like meaningless information. If however we read it as a part of the book of Second Timothy then immediately it is obvious that this is an instruction from Paul to Timothy, we also see that Paul is in prison expecting to face the death penalty. Reading further, perhaps an introduction to the book we learn that Timothy is a

---

1 2 Timothy 4:13

close friend and associate of Paul's, that Nero was the Emperor, and that Christians in Rome faced persecution. Our understanding becomes fleshed out, we begin to picture Paul, an old man, leader of the first century church, shivering (without his cloak) in a Roman jail cell. We can come to appreciate the risks for Timothy in associating with him, as well as Paul's own faith in the face of his imminent death.

The same is true when we come to grapple with a hard passage, or a contradiction. Understanding, to some degree both the literary and historical contexts will help us know what is being communicated. In some cases merely reading the paragraph or the entire chapter exposes the seeming contradiction as an invention, a deliberate misunderstanding. In all cases a thorough understanding promotes an informed discussion.

Different Types of Literature

Although we may not use the terminology everyone is familiar with the concept of different types of literature. For example if a person picks up a novel there is a certain way they will approach that type of writing; it will be read from beginning to end, probably for entertainment, and it will generally be assumed that the contents are fictional. However, pick up a telephone directory and everything changes! How we read the phone book, as well as why is completely different! Take a newspaper and there are differences once again. Being familiar with the different types of writing that surround us, help us to know how to understand them.

The same issues confront us when we open the Bible. Some types of literature, such as the letters, are easy for us to understand. Others, perhaps prophetic oracles, are totally unlike anything we have read before and tend to leave us bewildered. Therefore, for us to read the Bible with understanding, to know for example whether a passage was intended by its author to be literal or figurative, we must acquire some level of familiarity with the different types of literature found within the Bible.

Imagine someone from a world where the only type of literature they ever came in contact with was the news. How would they relate to a novel? More to the point, because of their background, it is to be expected that they would regard the contents of the novel as fact. If someone had only ever read novels, would they know what to do with a telephone book? If someone has only read western literature produced during the last few centuries, as well as other contemporary media (news, letters, documentaries etc), will he or she know how to read middle eastern literature produced three thousand years ago? It will be a struggle! There will be unfamiliar modes of expression, figures of speech, and literary devices. And so because of these differences, for us to be informed readers of the Bible, to understand if there is indeed a contradiction, it is going to be important to develop some familiarity with the types of writing found within Scripture (see appendix 'Types of Literature' p85).

Contradiction or Something I don't Understand?

Sometimes what appears to be a contradiction is in fact a lack of understanding. There is in fact a reasonable explanation, I just may not know what it is. My lack of understanding however, does not alter the reality. The quadratic formula, $ax^2+bx+c=0$ may seem like nonsense at first, but if I am willing to put in the effort I will come to appreciate its truth. Do we really expect God's revelation about himself to be entirely simple? To not at times stretch and even surpass our thinking. Most 'contradictions' are cleared up with a little further thought. However, when considering God himself there will be other difficulties; places in Scripture where we glimpse the heart and mind of God, and are forced to acknowledge that he is beyond us.

If anyone is truly interested in discussing difficulties, in the Bible or anywhere else, serious thinking will be required! Real life is complicated, it can be hard to understand, we have to work at it. Knowing the Bible, will be the best thing you can do in preparing yourself to talk about hard passages.

It should also be mentioned that not believing something to be true does not make it a contradiction or an error. The Gospel writers all record the resurrection of Jesus from the dead. From the perspective of internal consistency there is no contradiction within the Bible on this topic. However, some will say that this and other miracles are themselves examples of Bible errors. It may be helpful to make a distinction between a claim that someone finds hard to accept as true; and something that appears actually inconsistent.

Which was Created First, Animals or People?

References: Genesis 1:25-26 and Genesis 2:18-19

Type of Contradiction: Differing Accounts

The Claim: In Genesis chapter one we are told that the animals were created before human beings, but Genesis chapter two says that people were created first.

Key Points to Consider:

- The author of these chapters may not have intended them to be structured along strict chronological lines.
- Each chapter looks at creation from a different perspective.

A Response:

Each chapter tells the creation story with a different focus. In the first we have a grand overview of God's action of creation, here humanity is the culmination of God's work. With chapter two the perspective is more intimate. The entire focus of this second account is on humanity within God's creation.

It must also be noted that a careful reading of chapter two may dispel the claim of contradiction altogether! *'Then the LORD God said, "It is not good that the man should be alone; I will make him a helper fit for him."*

*Now out of the ground the LORD God **had** formed every beast of the field and every bird of the heavens...'*[2] Although man is

[2] Genesis 2:18-19a

mentioned here before the animals, they are mentioned in the past tense, God had created them already. From the original language this is not absolutely clear, some scholars believe the words used indicate future tense, others past.

Finally it must be noted that for modern westerners a strict chronological structure is almost always favoured. However, this was not the case for the ancient Hebrews. The author of Genesis may mention humanity once after and then once before the animals because it both suited his purpose and fitted within the accepted literary conventions of his day. He is not trying to deceive us regarding who came first, possibly he is not commenting on that at all.

Was God Satisfied with Creation?

References: Genesis 1:31 and Genesis 6:6

Type of Contradiction: Contrary Statements

The Claim: Genesis chapter one ends with God seeing all that he had made, and proclaiming it to be very good. However, Genesis 6:6 expresses an entirely different sentiment, here God regrets his creation of humanity.

Key Points to Consider:

- Strictly speaking there is no actual contradiction, God makes a good world and later regrets the evil actions of humanity.

A Response:

In Genesis chapters one and two we see God's creation of the world. At this point things were good! However, the untouched goodness of creation did not remain as God intended it to be for long. In Genesis chapter three humanity rebels against God with the consequence that sin, death, sickness and suffering enter into the created world.

By chapter six human beings have made such a mess of themselves and God's world that it pains him. The expression of God's regret found in chapter six does not in some way mean that the world wasn't good, rather it is an expression of the pain God feels in seeing that goodness so spoiled.

Does God get Tired?

References: Genesis 2:2 and Isaiah 40:28

Type of Contradiction: Contrary Statements

The Claim: In Genesis we see that God rests after he finishes creating the world. However, Isaiah 40:28 says that God doesn't grow weary.

Key Points to Consider:

- There is no explicit contradiction between these verses.
- It is possible that God ceased working for reasons other than being tired.

A Response:

Isaiah 40:28 is a part of a section of Isaiah were the prophet is telling the people of the greatness of God. Isaiah's point is that God is totally without equal, he is greater than any other so called god and the people of Israel should put their faith in him.

Genesis 2:2 concludes the account of God's creation of the world. We are told that for six days God created and then rested on the seventh. The text does not say that God was tired, it doesn't say why he rested at all. Most people assume that God rested because his work of creation was complete. There was nothing more for him to do, this rest was a celebration of the completion of creation

There really is no contradiction between these two verses. Isaiah tells us of the greatness of God. Genesis speaks of the completion of God's creation of the world.

Does the Bible Value Women?

References: Genesis 3:16, 1st Corinthians 14:34, Judges 4 and Luke 10:39

Type of Contradiction: Contrary Statements

The Claim: Some Biblical passages seem to imply that women are inferior to men, but others seem to say that men and women are equal.

Key Points to Consider:

- 21st century readers live in a very different world then the characters found within Biblical narratives, sometimes it is not immediately clear whether a statement is implying inferiority or not.

- There are numerous instances within the Bible where woman have roles of prominence, both in religious and secular matters. Nowhere is there any direct or implicit statement that these women behaved inappropriately.

A Response:

The Bible is absolutely in favour of women and seeks to confer on them the same status and value as men. Throughout the histories of Israel and the early Christian church women enjoyed positions of authority serving as judges, prophets, wise people and church leaders.

Despite this there are still a number of passages that we find difficult. For example, in Genesis, God speaking to Eve says, *'he (your husband) shall rule over you'.*[3] If we read not just that verse but the surrounding paragraphs we see that humanity has rebelled against God and now God is telling them what will happen because of this rebellion. In Genesis three God is not telling Eve what he wants to happen, but what will happen. A man ruling his wife is right alongside the ground producing thistles and death entering the human race; this is not something that God ever wanted! He is essentially saying that the typical man is physically stronger than the typical women, and there will be times when men abuse that strength. Again this is something that happens because some men behave badly, it is not God's heart for women!

1st Corinthians 14:34-35 says, *'the women should keep silent in the churches. For they are not permitted to speak, but should be in submission, as the Law also says. If there is anything they desire to learn, let them ask their husbands at home. For it is shameful for a woman to speak in church.'* Modern readers are understandably shocked by a passage like this! However, it must be remembered that Paul was not writing to us, but to the churches in the ancient city of Corinth. This is not a command for all women at all times, in all places; reading the whole of first Corinthians we can see that it's not even a command for all of the women, at all times during a Corinthian church service; elsewhere Paul instructs these women regarding how they are to speak to the church. Rather, what we have here seems to have been a very disorderly church, everyone seems to have talked (or shouted) at once, there was eating, and drinking, essentially

---

3 Genesis 3:16

you get the sense that they were swinging from the chandeliers, loud, raucous and utterly chaotic. Female church goers were being encouraged to learn (probably for the first time in their lives), and in the general atmosphere of chaos these ladies where shouting their questions from one side of the building to the other. Paul is concerned that their services were wildly off putting to outsiders, and that church members were missing out on the teaching they had come to hear because of the prevalent party atmosphere. Into this situation Paul tells them to do a number of things differently, one of which is to have the women ask questions about the sermon at home.

It should be noted that women being encouraged to learn anything beyond domestic tasks was extremely rare within the first century Roman world. Acceptance of women was something that the early church was known (and despised) for. Repeatedly within Paul's letters to the churches women are encouraged to learn, pray and prophesy. Jesus also had female disciples, and within the early church leadership there were female apostles.

How Many Animals were on the Ark?

References: Genesis 7:2 and Genesis 7:9

Type of Contradiction: Differing Accounts

The Claim: In verse two we are told that Noah was to take seven pairs of all the clean animals onto the ark, and one pair of the unclean animals. However, in verse nine we are told that the animals went into the ark, *'two and two, male and female'*[4]. We are left with the question, was it two of every animal, or fourteen of some?

Key Points to Consider:

- The mention of the animals going into the ark in pairs (verse nine) does not comment on how many pairs of each species were involved.

A Response:

It seems that with verse two we have more information. Specifically that for some kinds of animals God commanded Noah to bring more than one pair. Being told a few verses later that the animals entered the ark in male / female pairs does not have to imply that there was only a single pair taken of each species.

In chapter six Noah is also commanded by God to bring a pair of every sort of animal onto the ark. It seems entirely reasonable to assume that in touching on the subject the author feels free to

---

4 Genesis 7:9a

speak of animals in pairs; whilst at other times he feels the need to go into greater detail, explicitly stating just how many pairs of each species were being taken on board.

Should Men be Circumcised?

References: Genesis 17:10 and Galatians 5:2

Type of Contradiction: Contrary Statements

The Claim: In Genesis God commands Abraham and his male descendants to be circumcised, but in Galatians Christians are told they should not be circumcised.

Key Points to Consider:

- The people of Israel under their ancient law code were commanded to circumcise male Israelites.
- Nowhere does the Bible command Christians to be circumcised.
- The issue of circumcision is dealt with explicitly and at some length in the New Testament.

A Response:

Circumcision was commanded as an outward sign for members of the Old Testament Covenant Community, the people of the ancient nation of Israel. In New Testament times many Christians (with an Israeli background) felt that anyone who became a Christian should be circumcised. In effect there was a desire to carry on this outward sign, as well as other aspects of the Old Testament Israeli law. Because of this, very early in Church history the question was asked, 'Is circumcision something that Christian men need to undergo?' People wanted to know whether God's command to Abraham regarding the circumcision of his descendants should be carried over to all people who came to believe in God. Put another way, according to the Bible, can one be a Christian man, and not be circumcised?

The conclusions reached by the early church leaders was that Christians did not need to be circumcised, faith in Jesus was what counted. *'For in Christ Jesus neither circumcision nor uncircumcision counts for anything, but only faith working through love.'*[5]

The Bible commanded the ancient people of Israel to be circumcised, but does not command that Christians follow the same practise.

---

5 Galatians 5:6

Who were the Fathers of the Twelve Tribes of Israel?

References: Genesis 49:2-28 and Revelation 7:4-8

Type of Contradiction: Contrary Statements

The Claim: Genesis lists the Fathers of the twelve tribes as: Reuben, Simeon, Levi, Judah, Zebulun, Issachar, Dan, Gad, Asher, Naphtali, Joseph, and Benjamin. However, Revelation omits Dan and adds Manasseh.

Key Points to Consider:

- Strictly speaking, neither of these references list the twelve tribes of Israel. Genesis lists the twelve sons of Jacob, and Revelation contains a figurative list intended to convey a picture of the people of God.

- Because Jacob adopted Joseph's sons (his grandsons) as his own there were thirteen tribes in total.

A Response:

The sons of Jacob were; Reuben, Simeon, Levi, Judah, Zebulun, Issachar, Dan, Gad, Asher, Naphtali, Joseph, and Benjamin. However, these were not quite the twelve tribes of Israel. In speaking of twelve tribes, Levi is generally not counted (they were given no land), and Joseph is in effect counted twice through his sons Ephraim and Manasseh.

Genesis therefore lists the sons of Jacob, for a list of the twelve tribes both Levi and Joseph's names would be removed and replaced with Ephraim and Manasseh. Revelation differs because the author does not want us to believe he is listing people from the literal (and by his time largely lost) twelve tribes, he is using imagery to describe those who follow God.

So, neither reference is intended to name the fathers of the tribes of Israel. For a list of the twelve tribes as they functioned throughout the history of ancient Israel see Numbers chapter one.

The God of War or the God of Peace?

References: Exodus 15:3 and Romans 15:33

Type of Contradiction: Contrary Statements

The Claim: Exodus 15:3 describes God as a man of war, and elsewhere in the Bible God appears warlike. However, in Romans 15:33, and elsewhere, God is the God of peace. Which is it?

Key Points to Consider:

- Perhaps God at different times, and in different places can be both.

A Response:

As human beings we find ourselves being many different things, or perhaps we could say there are different facets to who we are. You might be a mother, sister, an employee, and a friend. Similarly, depending on the situation you might be calm, angry, rushed, excited or frustrated. Isn't it possible for God to advocate war in one situation, and peace in another? As the sovereign creator and ruler of the universe I believe that he can be both of these things, they are not mutually exclusive.

Is it Okay to Kill?

References: Exodus 20:13 and Exodus 32:27

Type of Contradiction: Contrary Statements

The Claim: Exodus chapter twenty gives the Ten Commandments, one of which is a prohibition against murder. However, in chapter thirty two God commands that certain people be killed.

Key Points to Consider:

- Not all killing can legitimately be classified as murder (e.g. an accidental death).
- Those that God commands to be put to death in chapter thirty two had committed a capital offence under the laws of their nation.

A Response:

When we consider the killing of one human being by another there are a number of broad categories into which that killing may fall. Certainly one of those is murder, generally defined as a malicious and unlawful killing. However, even then, legal systems tend to make a distinction between premeditated murder, and murder carried out in anger on the spur of the moment. A killing might not be murder at all, on occasion it will be the result of an accident. Still other killings occur during times of war, and others are carried out by executioners at the bidding of the legal system. So not every act of killing can be defined as a murder.

Exodus chapter twenty does not talk about killing in general, it only deals with murder. In this chapter it is murder that is forbidden (offenders received the death penalty). In Exodus thirty two murder does not come up at all; in that passage a group of people had become involved in the worship of other gods, a capital offence under ancient Israeli law. They are sentenced to death for their actions. It would be a misleading simplification of the facts to merely state that one verse promotes and another prohibits killing.

Is it Okay to Lie?

References: Exodus 20:16, Proverbs 12:22, James 2:25 and 1st Samuel 16:1-2

Type of Contradiction: Contrary Statements

The Claim: Exodus twenty prohibits lying, as one of the ten commandments; further Proverbs twelve says that it is an abomination. Yet, James says that Rahab's lie was commendable and God himself seems to be telling Samuel to lie to Saul!

Key Points to consider:

- Exodus condemns not so much lying in general, as perjury.
- God does not actually tell Samuel to lie, rather not to reveal the whole truth.
- Proverbs twelve verses twenty two gives a contrast between practises God loves and hates, dishonesty on one hand, trustworthiness on the other.

A Response:

The Proverb's reference would seem to clearly tell us that God expects honesty. If we are in any doubt we could consider Jesus' words, in condemning the need for oaths he exhorts his listeners to simply say yes or no and be bound by that alone. We might think of this as honouring all of our verbal agreements, not merely legal contracts. The message is maintain honesty at all times!

Rahab was a Canaanite prostitute who lied to help some Israelite spies escape capture. James tells us that this act showed her faith in the God of Israel. Strictly speaking Rahab is not praised for lying so much as her faith in God. True, that faith was made evident when she lied to the authorities, but it is her faith, not her dishonesty that is commended.

First Samuel doesn't actually contain lying, however, it does look very much as though God himself is directing Samuel to mislead Saul. "'*I will send you to Jesse the Bethlehemite, for I have provided for myself a king among his sons." And Samuel said, "How can I go? If Saul hears it, he will kill me." And the Lord said, "Take a heifer with you and say, "I have come to sacrifice to the Lord.*'"[6] Strictly speaking God is not telling Samuel to lie, rather, he instructs him not to tell the whole truth to Saul. The question then becomes, 'was Saul entitled to know the whole truth?'

The example from the book of Samuel is extreme, it concerns dealings with a dictatorship willing to kill on a suspicion of disloyalty. As a whole the Bible tells us clearly not to lie, to speak honestly; however there are times when we are not obliged to reveal the whole truth.

---

6 1st Samuel 16:1b-2

An Eye for an Eye, or Turn the Other Cheek?

References: Exodus 21:23-25 and Matthew 5:38-44

Type of Contradiction: Contrary Statements

The Claim: Exodus teaches that when a person is wronged there should be retribution. However, in Mathew's Gospel Jesus urges his followers not to retaliate at all.

Key Points to Consider:

- The law code of Exodus is not stipulating retribution so much as limiting the forms it may take.
- Jesus, in the Sermon on the Mount doesn't so much disagree as take the point made in Exodus a step further.
- These two statements were given to different groups of people.

A Response:

In Exodus, a part of ancient Israel's legal code, the stipulation is given that punishment for wrong doing should not be disproportionate with regard to the original offence. The point to note is that Exodus is about limiting, not demanding vengeance. In the ancient world this was a significant step forward. If a person was wronged or hurt in some way Exodus does not permit him to strike back with excessive force. We might think of this as letting the punishment fit the crime. If for example a wealthy man was cheated out of a flock of six sheep he may want to ruin the man who cheated him. Exodus tells both the rich man, as well as the judge deciding his case that while he is entitled to be compensated for what he lost, he isn't allowed to go beyond this.

The law of Exodus isn't demanding an eye for an eye, it is saying that is the upper limit. Exodus says, if someone damages your eye, you are entitled to seek reasonable compensation, but you are not allowed to kill that person. This law prevents vengeance or the demands for compensation from being taken too far. Jesus, in Matthew's gospel, takes it a step further. He tells his listeners, that when wronged they are to forgive. He urges us to lay down any right to seek compensation, or revenge whatsoever.

These two references are not saying contrary things, both point in the same direction, however Jesus leads his listeners a step further. The aim of both is to promote forgiveness over revenge and bitterness.

Did God want Burnt Offerings?

References: Leviticus 1:9 (and elsewhere) and Isaiah 1:11

Type of Contradiction: Contrary Statements

The Claim: Leviticus both in one verse nine and throughout much of the book stresses the importance of making proper offerings and sacrifices to God. Yet in Isaiah one verse eleven God does not seem to care about sacrifices at all.

Key Points to Consider:

- The offerings were never the whole picture, in God's eyes the state of someone's heart was always more important than a technically correct offering.

A Response:

The sacrificial system, set up to a large degree within the book of Leviticus was not intended to be the whole picture. Jesus described the heart of this system as loving God and loving other people (those questioning him agreed). And so God always expected more than the actual act of sacrifice. The sacrifices were meant to be accompanied by a heart attitude; yes the people were meant to be faithfully performing their acts of communal worship, but they were also meant to be loving each other.

Hundreds of years later we come to the time of the prophet Isaiah. The sacrifices were still, to some degree happening, but the people were not living right. Isaiah is saying 'you have missed the point!' You can not mistreat one another, mechanically perform a sacrifice, and believe God is okay with that! Isaiah begs them to remember the heart of the sacrificial system.

Should Men Have Long Hair?

References: Numbers 6:5 and 1st Corinthians 11:14

Type of Contradiction: Contrary Statements

The Claim: The author of Numbers seems to present men wearing their hair long hair as a positive thing, but the author of 1st Corinthians says it is a disgrace.

Key Points to Consider:

- Numbers commends long hair (or rather abstaining from cutting the hair) as part of the Nazarite vow. This was a time that a man (or woman) could set aside to focus themselves on God, uncut hair was a visible sign that someone was in the midst of their Nazarite vow.

- 1st Corinthians was written to the church within the Greek city of Corinth in about AD 55. Some members of this church were adopting standards of dress and behaviour (such as men growing their hair) that were offensive or regarded as inappropriate by others within their city.

A Response:

Firstly it must be noted that long hair (for men) is neither universally commanded or condemned. Under ancient Israeli law there was a prohibition against cutting the hair during a Nazarite vow, which for some, those who choose to live as Nazarites for a long time, would lead to long hair. 1st Corinthians does not deal with Nazarite vows or anything similar. Certain members of the

Corinthian church were behaving in such a way that their non-church going neighbours found them offensive. Because of this the Apostle Paul tells them in essence, 'Don't cause trouble for no reason, don't upset or offend people!' First century Greek culture said that men should have short hair and women long, Paul tells the Christians in Corinth to go along with this.

So the Bible says that sometimes a man's hair should be long, at other times and places he should cut it short; that in itself is not contradictory. Different behaviours and standards of dress are entirely appropriate in different settings.

Does God Change His Mind?

References: Numbers 23:19 and Jonah 3:10 (as well as others too numerous to list)

Type of Contradiction: Contrary Statements

The Claim: In some passages it seems that God changes his mind as the situation develops, or in response to someone's prayer. However, in other passages it is very clearly stated that God does not change his mind.

Key Points to Consider:

- Attempting to understand how God operates, even in part, will stretch and surpass our mental abilities.
- There are numerous Biblical passages that could be used to say either God never changes, or that he sometimes does; both sides need to be considered in dealing with this contradiction.

A Response:

This is an area of interest for many people, it quickly goes beyond, 'does God change his mind?' to 'are our choices real?'.

On the one hand we have a whole collection of Scripture references that clearly tell us God does not change, he will do what he has said he will do, he knows the end from the beginning, and that he is in control of all of history. If this was all that was said about God then it would be easy for us to think that our choices are of no consequence, even that we don't really have any choices at all. If God knows everything that will ever happen then we must be trapped within his all powerful will.

On the other hand there are also references within Scripture where we see people praying, or repenting, and huge changes seem to occur. Not to mention numerous accounts of God holding people accountable for the choices that they make, either good or bad.

So which is it? Both; the Bible, as a whole clearly teaches us that God is in control of all of history, down to the smallest details. But also that our choices are real, important, and that our prayers matter.

How can that be correct? How can both be true? I don't know; but then, whether I am able to understand how something works is not the real factor in determining its validity. A believer is probably willing to accept that God is beyond him or her, that as human beings we are not able to fully understand the creator. The unbeliever may be inclined to think this is rubbish, a clear error within the Bible dishonestly glossed over. From that perspective just suppose for a minute that there is a God out there. A God whose abilities in every area eclipse your own immeasurably. Whose existence goes beyond and outside of time, whose intellect is completely beyond our own, whose power and creative genius you can barely begin to guess at. If he chose to reveal something of himself to you, would you expect to completely understand it? Surely there would be times, and areas that were both absolutely true, and absolutely beyond your grasp.

Three God's or One?

References: Deuteronomy 6:4 and Genesis 1:26

Type of Contradiction: Contrary Statements

The Claim: Deuteronomy six specifically states that there is only one God, however, in Genesis one God refers to himself as 'we'. Is there one God, several, or a multitude?

Key Points to Consider:

- If there is an all powerful creator God we as a part of his creation will not understand everything about him.
- By we get to the New Testament there is more information, God is described as Father, Son and Holy Spirit.

A Response:

Jews, Christians and Moslems are regarded as monotheists. That is people who believe there is only one true God. So taking the belief in one God as the starting point what do we make of Genesis one, verse twenty six, not to mention the New Testament?

Some have thought that Genesis could be written in what we might think of as 'court language'. That is in using the pronoun, 'we' God includes the heavenly court in this statement. Others have seen this as an early pointer towards the doctrine of the Trinity.

The word Trinity is never mentioned in the Bible, but taking everything that the Bible says about who God is led people to this idea. Specifically, that God is one, and also three. That there is one God, but then there is in some sense also God the Father, God the Son, and God the Holy Spirit.

The concept of the Trinity is not something that human beings have been able to understand fully. However, that does not make it incorrect or contradictory. It just means that God is beyond us.

If Anger is Wrong, Why is God Sometimes Angry?

References: Deuteronomy 6:15 and Matthew 5:22

Type of Contradiction: Contrary Statements

The Claim: In Deuteronomy, as well as elsewhere within the Bible we see God talk about his own anger. However, Matthew 5:22 says that anyone who is angry with his brother is liable to be judged. So anger is portrayed as a bad thing.

Key Points to Consider:

- Not all anger is the same, sometimes there is what we might consider reasonable provocation, sometimes not. Further when a person becomes angry there is a wide range of possible behaviours ranging from discussion to violent behaviour.

- The Bible teaches that God is perfect, that he doesn't do wrong things, and so presumably the emotion of anger itself is not wrong. Ephesians 4:26 would also support this view, here the Bible urges people to guard against doing the wrong thing under the influence of anger.

A Response:

In Matthew's Gospel Jesus is showing humanity God's standards. In this example, specifically, he says that not only is it wrong to murder, it is wrong to entertain murderous thoughts. Not only is it wrong to lose your temper and kill someone, it is wrong to lose your temper and fly into a rage.

Taking what the Bible says as a whole, anger is actually sometimes an appropriate response. Mistreatment of the vulnerable should cause us to feel anger, and provoke us to take appropriate action. However, once we are angry our perspective often becomes distorted and we may be inclined to take things too far. So the Bible also warns against excessive and prolonged anger.

God is at times angry when faced with injustices, anger itself is not denounced as wrong. On rare occasions anger is a right response. However, for human beings the Bible urges caution, and rebukes out of control rage.

Which Animals Should be Eaten?

References: Deuteronomy 14:7-8 and Acts 10:9-16

Type of Contradiction: Contrary Statements

The Claim: In Deuteronomy God tells the people of Israel which animals they can eat and which they can not, however, in Acts Peter is told to disregard the food laws altogether.

Key Points to Consider:

- The food laws in Deuteronomy were part of the legal system for the ancient people of Israel.

A Response:

The food laws of the Old Testament were given to the ancient nation of Israel as a part of their legal code. This law code was given to a specific group of people for a specific time period, it is not binding on everyone. In Acts Peter was being made aware of this; the vision of chapter ten is God making it clear to him that he is no longer bound by the Old Testament laws. This is not so much an issue of contradiction, as different laws being given to different people at different times in history.

Does God Judge People for the Sins of Their Parents?

References: Isaiah 14:21 and Deuteronomy 24:16

Type of Contradiction: Contrary Statements

The Claim: Deuteronomy 24:16 says that parents are not to be put to death because of their children's crimes, and vice versa. Isaiah 14:21 flies in the face of that command; here it is said that sons will be slaughtered because of their father's guilt.

Key Points to Consider:

- There are a number of other passages (e.g. Exodus 24:7 and Ezekiel 18) that also deal with these issues, looking at them may increase our understanding of this contradiction.
- Deuteronomy is the law given by God for the ancient nation of Israel, the reference above limits the types of punishments their judiciary could mete out. Isaiah chapter 14 is God saying what he will do in judgement of a wicked nation. Do Deuteronomy 24's limitations apply to God?
- Taking the Isaiah reference in isolation the reader does leave with the idea that the sons who were about to be punished were innocent. Broader reading reveals that both the sons (assuming them to be those living when Babylon fell to Persia) and their fathers were guilty and deserving of judgement.

A Response:

Beginning with Deuteronomy, *'Fathers shall not be put to death because of their children, nor shall children be put to death because of their fathers. Each one shall be put to death for his own sin.'*[7] Here we have something roughly akin to a constitutional right for ancient Israelites. When a crime is committed the punishment must be brought against the criminal, not one of his relatives. In contrast the Hammurabi code (a second millennium law code from Mesopotamia) stipulated that if someone's negligence caused the death of another man's son, then the negligent man's son was to be executed. This was not to happen in Israel. The person who committed the act of negligence was to bear the punishment. This passage is about individual responsibility.

Ezekiel chapter 18 also talks about the responsibility of individuals. However, Ezekiel is not law code, here God is telling the people (in some detail!) how he will judge them. They are explicitly told that if a man is righteous then he is righteous, God regards that man as righteous even if his father was evil, and his son becomes evil. Ezekiel chapter 18 was written at a time when the people were saying, 'we are innocent, God is judging us not for our sins, but for the sins of our parents.' God is very clear in refuting that thinking!

So, how does that line up with references such as Isaiah 14:21, *'Prepare slaughter for his sons because of the guilt of their fathers,'*[8]? This verse is part of a prophecy of judgement on the

---

7 Deuteronomy 24:16

nation of Babylon. The language is poetic, it does not seem as though we are talking about a specific father (or fathers) and specific sons. In Old Testament times people attached great importance to both children and their own burial, this was their legacy. In the previous verses the nation of Babylon has been told that it will not have a proper burial, and in verse 21 that it's children will also be destroyed. This is figurative language, Isaiah is saying that Babylon will be ruined and left without a memorial. Isaiah 14 is not talking about sons judged for their father's guilt at all.

The weight of Scripture tells us that we are each responsible for our own sin, and hence each of us must turn to Jesus. However, we do also see that the sins of others do affect us. In this life we may face difficulties because of the unrighteousness of others, but God holds us eternally accountable for ourselves.

8 Isaiah 14:21a

Did David Kill Goliath with a Sling or a Sword?

References: 1st Samuel 17:50 and 17:51

Type of Contradiction: Differing Accounts

The Claim: Strangely the author of Samuel says that David killed Goliath with a sling, but then in the next sentence that it was with a sword. It reads as though David killed Goliath twice!

Key Points to Consider:

- Verse 50 is a summary of the combat of David and Goliath, the reader is told that David triumphed over Goliath without a sword. It could perhaps be seen as something of a parenthesis.
- Verse 50 does say that David struck and killed Goliath. However, the verse is not explicit here, it is a matter of interpretation, did he strike him with sling or sword?
- Stepping back, looking at the chapter as a whole the chronology of events does seem clear.

A Response:

As mentioned above, although verse 50 is not completely clear, reading the chapter leaves us in no doubt as to what happened. In brief; Goliath challenged the Israelites to decide the battle through single combat, their champion against him. David accepts the challenge, uses his sling to incapacitate Goliath, and then kills him with Goliath's own sword.

These points, with a lot more detail make up the majority of 1st Samuel chapter 17. I do not think verse 50 (which in the narrative appears between David wounding Goliath with his sling, and killing him with a sword) is the result of confusion or intended to contradict the rest of the account. Rather, verse 50 is an outburst of excitement! The author is impressed with David! Impressed that he challenged Goliath and beat him and hadn't even brought a sword to the fight! After expressing these thoughts he resumes his narrative.

Who Tempted David? God or Satan?

References: 2nd Samuel 24:1 and 1st Chronicles 21:1

Type of Contradiction: Differing Accounts

The Claim: Both narratives describe a time during his reign when David takes a census of the people, and in doing so incurs the wrath of God. However, in 1st Samuel the author says that it was God who incited David, whereas Chronicles claims it was Satan.

Key Points to Consider:

- The author of Chronicles wrote some time after the author of Samuel, and was most likely familiar with the Samuel version of events, yet still chose to say Satan incited David.
- Each author wrote to a different audience and sought to present a different perspective.

A Response:

Probably what we have here is more a reflection of the different cultures than any sort of error. The Israelites during the Old Testament period had a very high view of God's sovereignty. He being all powerful could choose to stop any event. So if something, (anything) happened; God must have let it happen. In their eyes, God allowing something to happen, was essentially the same as him doing it, because nothing could happen against his will.

However, hundreds of years later when Chronicles was written there was a more complex understanding, and a greater interest in the supernatural world. These readers wanted to know precisely how something happened, they still accepted God's sovereignty but they also wanted the details.

Bearing this in mind, it seems that it was actually the Devil who incited David to take this census. The author of Samuel, attributes it to God because God allowed it. The author of Chronicles attributes it to Satan because he was more interested in the details. However, both had the same fundamental understanding of what had happened.

Is God Slow to Anger?

References: Psalm 103:8 and Jeremiah 17:4

Type of Contradiction: Contrary Statements

The Claim: Psalm one hundred and three paints the picture of a loving God, who is slow to become angry. Jeremiah seventeen on the other hand describes God's anger as a fire *'that shall burn forever'*.[9]

Key Points to Consider:

- There is no explicit contradiction between these verses.
- The reference in Jeremiah is describing God's anger, however, from both Jeremiah and the historical books covering this period (Kings and Chronicles) it is very clear that God has been slow to become angry.

A Response:

In Psalm one hundred and three we have something of a description of who God is. Specifically from verse eight we learn that he is slow to become angry, and that his graciousness and mercy outweigh his anger. This is further clarified in the following verses: *'He will not always chide, nor will he keep his anger forever. He does not deal with us according to our sins'.*[10]

---

9 Jeremiah 17:4

10 Psalm 103:9-10a

Jeremiah, together with the narratives of Kings and Chronicles, gives us a glimpse of that being worked out in history. Reading those books we see God's slowness to anger being demonstrated over a period of hundreds of years. However, by Jeremiah's life time things have become desperate. The people ignore God's final appeals for them to return to him, and so judgement is coming. Reading on in chapter seventeen we see Jeremiah make an appeal to God to be merciful, God listens to him; however the people reject God's mercy.

The Bible consistently portrays God as slow to become angry and quick to show kindness. Even when God does become angry he is quick to forgive.

Is it Folly to be Wise?

References: Proverbs 4:7 and Ecclesiastes 1:18

Type of Contradiction: Contrary Statements

The Claim: Proverbs says *'Get wisdom'*[11] and continues on for some verses expounding on the value of wisdom. The author of Proverbs clearly sees wisdom as worth seeking, but the author of Ecclesiastes seems to view wisdom with considerable negativity. Ecclesiastes 1:18 says that wisdom will lead to vexation and sorrow.

Key Points to Consider:

- These two books were written with different purposes in mind.
- It is conceivable that in some situations wisdom will be beneficial and in others frustrating.

A Response:

These passages are talking about very different things! Understanding of the broader context goes a very long way in explaining these statements.

Proverbs is talking about wisdom in terms of living intelligently. The exhortation to pursue wisdom is in the context of a father's advice for successful living, given to his child.

---

11 Proverbs 4:7

Ecclesiastes on the other hand is talking about the failure of human wisdom in giving purpose to life. The author is on a journey of discovery, wisdom is where he begins, however being wise does not give him satisfaction. His own wisdom did not answer life's hard questions, merely deepened his desire for those answers.

In Proverbs wisdom is being talked about as worthwhile and helpful. A beneficial aspect of a successful life. In Ecclesiastes the author has entirely different concerns! Here wisdom is not about living well, but answering questions about the meaning of life altogether. For the first task wisdom is adequate (the author of Ecclesiastes acknowledges this too), but for the later, human wisdom is out of its depth. These statements are not contradicting each other, they are merely talking about different things.

Is it Okay to Drink Alcohol?

References: Proverbs 31:6-7, 1st Timothy 5:23, Proverbs 20:1 and Proverbs 23:31-32

Type of Contradiction: Contrary Statements

The Claim: Writing to Timothy, Paul urges him to drink 'a little wine', Proverbs thirty one also advocates giving wine to people in distress. However, Proverbs twenty and twenty three both view wine with some negativity.

Key Points to Consider:

- Strictly speaking, drinking of alcohol is nowhere forbidden in the Bible.
- In a number of passages excessive alcohol consumption is condemned.

A Response:

Within the Bible we find some instances where the consumption of alcohol is advised; as well as many other passages that warn people against too much alcohol. Taking them all into account there is no actual contradiction, broadly speaking the Bible tells us that it is okay to drink alcohol, as long as your consumption is moderate.

Who was the Father of Joseph?

References: Matthew 1:16 and Luke 3:23

Type of Contradiction: Differing Accounts

The Claim: The Bible disagrees with itself on who the father of Joseph, (and therefore legal grandfather of Jesus) was. Specifically, the Gospels of Matthew and Luke both contain genealogies ending with Jesus. However these genealogies are significantly different; Matthew lists Jacob as Jesus' paternal grandfather, but Luke tells us the father of Joseph was in fact Heli.

Key Points to Consider:

- Ancient genealogies were not written strictly as a registry of births and deaths, skipping generations was common practice.

- The word translated 'father' can also mean grandfather, ancestor or even predecessor.

A Response:

These genealogys differ on many points! In neither case do we have the sort of precision that as 21st century westerners we would expect. Important for us to realize is that in recording this type of genealogy ancient writers were quite happy to say that Tom was the father of Levi, where as in reality Tom was Levi's great grandfather. The word used can mean either son or descendant, even at times successor.

A particular genealogy may only record significant historical figures, or as in Matthew be grouped around a particular number. The genealogy was meant to show how we get from 'a' to 'z', mentioning everything in between was not as important to these authors.

With Matthew and Luke it has been suggested that Matthew has traced the royal line of David, presenting Jesus as David's heir. Luke on the other hand is thought to have given us something closer to the actual bloodline of Joseph.

Both author's wrote with a particular point; Matthew to show us Jesus, heir to the throne of David, Messiah of the Jews. Luke to show us Jesus the human being, saviour of all humanity. Neither included a genealogy so that we could see who Jesus' great-great grandparents were.

It must be remembered that the authors and first readers of these genealogies viewed them differently than we tend to. When they read something like this they come with different expectations, specifically, they did not expect a technically precise or complete list, generations may be skipped to suit the author's main purpose. Therefore, in the eyes of a first century Jew, both genealogies are accurate.

Was Jesus Born in House or Manger?

References: Matthew 2:11 and Luke 2:7

Type of Contradiction: Differing Accounts

The Claim: Matthew describes the wise men visiting Jesus, Mary and Joseph in a house, presumably shortly after Jesus' birth. Luke tells us that there was no accommodation available, and so following his birth (which presumably occurred in a stable or other animal shed) Mary placed Jesus in a manger. Was Jesus born in a house or a stable?

Key Points to Consider:

- While Luke clearly tells us that Jesus was born in a stable Matthew doesn't give a place of birth beyond the city of Bethlehem.
- The wise men may have visited Jesus weeks, months or even years after his birth, the time is not explicitly defined.

A Response:

Looking at what is said in both Matthew and Luke it seems that Mary and Joseph arrived in Bethlehem shortly before Jesus' birth. They failed to find accommodation immediately and so Jesus was born in an animal shelter. However, they did not live there permanently, it seems that Mary and Joseph soon found a house, and presumably employment and so decided to remain in Bethlehem. All of this could have been accomplished within a week!

Matthew does not tell us how much time passed between Jesus' birth and the arrival of the wise men. However, they were not the only ones looking for Jesus, Herod the King of Judea after hearing rumours of his birth was seeking to kill him. When King Herod realised that the wise men were not going to deliver Jesus to him he ordered the boys of Bethlehem two years old or less to be killed. It seems that Jesus may have been as old as two before the wise men visited him in a house.

There is no contradiction between Matthew and Luke on this matter. Jesus and his family merely moved from their very temporary accommodation in a stable, into a house some time before the wise men arrived to worship him.

Did John the Baptist Know that Jesus was the Messiah?

References: Matthew 3:11-14, John 1:29-34 and Matthew 11:2-3

Type of Contradiction: Contrary Statements

The Claim: In Matthew chapter three, and John chapter one John the Baptist essentially identifies Jesus as the Jewish Messiah (or at least someone special); however in Matthew chapter eleven he does not seem so sure, and sends people to ask Jesus who he is.

Key Points to Consider:

- Perhaps John thought Jesus was the Messiah, and then a few years later had some doubts.
- Strictly speaking these passages do not contain a contradiction.

A Response:

We have all, probably, seen or heard something extraordinary or surprising, and then perhaps moments later wondered, 'did that really just happen?' It doesn't seem unreasonable that John's experience was similar. I believe at Jesus' baptism God told John that Jesus was the Messiah, the long prophesied deliverer. John no doubt had his own expectations regarding what the Messiah would do. The years go by, John is in jail, the Messiah is not doing quite what John had expected; naturally he had questions! This is not a contradiction, but an honest description of John the Baptist's thoughts.

Where did Jesus Meet Peter and Andrew?

References: Matthew 4:18-19 and John 1:40-42

Type of Contradiction: Differing Accounts

The Claim: In Matthew's account Jesus first notices Peter and Andrew fishing by the Sea of Galilee, and it is here that he calls them to become his followers. However, in John's gospel readers are told that Andrew was first a follower of John the Baptist; that it was in fact John who encouraged Andrew to follow Jesus, and that Andrew then recruited Peter.

Key Points to Consider:

- Matthew records Jesus calling Peter and Andrew to become his followers, however Matthew does not claim that this scene by the Sea of Galilee was their first contact with Jesus.
- The two accounts are not mutually exclusive.
- John, writing decades after Matthew would presumably have been aware of Matthew's account, it does not seem he considered the two incompatible.

A Response:

Perhaps events could be reconstructed in this way: Andrew, both a fisherman, and person of faith became a follower of John the Baptist. Presumably during this time he continued to fish, but spent a considerable amount of time listening to the teachings of

John. During one such occasion he was encouraged by John to become a follower of Jesus.

At John's urging Andrew, together with his brother Peter then spent some time with Jesus. Perhaps this was a one off occasion, or perhaps there were several visits. All the while they both continue to earn their living as commercial fishermen. At some point Jesus then called them to leave fishing and to follow him full time.

It appears entirely plausible that John's gospel records the first meeting of Jesus with these two brothers, and Matthew's tells us when they accepted the call to follow him 'full time'.

Where Did Jesus Preach His Most Famous Sermon?

References: Matthew 5:1-2 and Luke 6:17

Type of Contradiction: Differing Accounts

The Claim: In Matthew's Gospel he records Jesus' famous 'Sermon on the Mount'. Luke records a very similar sermon, but says that Jesus delivered it from a plain.

Key Points to Consider:

- Perhaps Jesus gave two sermons, each to a different group, and each in different places.

A Response:

There are certainly noticeable similarities between these two accounts. However, there are also differences! Considerably more topics are covered in Matthew's 'Sermon on the Mount'. It seems entirely plausible that we have preserved here two separate sermons, with some content in common. It must be remembered that none of the Gospels tell us everything Jesus said or did. In this case it seems that of the four writers Matthew chose to include the 'Sermon on the Mount', Luke the 'Sermon on the Plain' and Mark and John did not record either of them.

Did the Centurion come to Jesus or send a Friend?

References: Matthew 8:5-12 and Luke 7:2-10

Type of Contradiction: Differing Accounts

The Claim: According to Matthew the Centurion came himself to ask Jesus for help, but in Luke's account he sends messengers to ask on his behalf.

Key Points to Consider:

- In both accounts Jesus dialogues with the Centurion, either directly or through intermediaries.
- While Luke gives more detail regarding the Centurion's interactions with Jesus, Matthew includes more of Jesus' words to those around him. Both authors, writing to different audiences seek to emphasize different points.

A Response:

These two accounts do not contradict one another, rather one is more condensed than the other.

Presumably Luke gives us the more precise details regarding what happened. That is a Centurion sent first some Jewish elders, and then some friends to ask a favour of Jesus. So in one sense the elders ask, but in another the Centurion does; they are representing him, acting on his behalf as messengers. Matthew does not feel that his purposes are served by going to this level of detail, and so he takes a step back and simply tells us of the interaction between Jesus and the Centurion. How that interaction was accomplished is less important.

Today we might call a friend and tell them something, or, as in this case ask someone to pass along a message. In either case that message still comes from us. This is essentially the difference of these accounts, one of detail not error.

How did Judas Die?

References: Matthew 27:3-10 and Acts 1:18-19

Type of Contradiction: Differing Accounts

The Claim: According to Matthew Judas committed suicide by hanging himself. Luke, the author of Acts tells us that Judas committed suicide by falling, with the added detail that his bowels came out.

Further, in Matthew's account it is the priests who buy the field; but according to Luke Judas buys the field.

Key Points to Consider:

- Each author wrote to a different audience and sought to emphasis different points. In his account Matthew seeks to show that Old Testament prophecy was fulfilled; Luke shows that wickedness does not pay off.
- Both Matthew and Luke agree on the central points; Judas betrayed Jesus, received a financial reward, and finally committed suicide.

A Response:

There are two issues to address here; firstly who purchased the field? Was it Judas himself, or the priests? Secondly, what was the manner of his death?

Matthew gives a more detailed record of events; Judas regrets his betrayal of Jesus, returns the thirty pieces of silver, and then commits suicide. Luke in a few words speaks of Judas acquiring a field. I believe that strictly speaking Matthew gives us the events as they occurred. Writing to a predominantly Jewish audience he may also have wanted to stress that Judas did not personally purchase property within the promised land (which would have been considered a blessing). Luke on the other hand, writing to Gentiles, does not face this concern. He may have felt free to say that Judas acquired the field because the money that went to its purchase was known to have been Judas' money.

The precise nature of Judas' death can not now be known. However, the two accounts are not necessarily opposed. When Judas hung himself it is not inconceivable that things ended messily!

Let's assume he intended to hang himself from a tree. He must have climbed to one of the higher branches, secured the noose, and jumped. It is possible that he tore himself in either the fall or through the failure of the rope.

Assuming that both Matthew and Luke knew precisely how Judas died; a hanging gone horribly wrong, it is not difficult to believe that they may have summed things up differently. Neither talks at length about Judas' suicide. A different selection of details does not necessarily mean a different event is being narrated.

What were Jesus' Last Words?

References: Matthew 27:45-50, Mark 15:33-37, Luke 23:46 and John 19:30

Type of Contradiction: Differing Accounts

The Claim: Matthew and Mark both tell us that Jesus' last words were, *'My God, my God, why have you forsaken me?'*[12]. However, Luke records Jesus saying, *'Father, into your hands I commit my spirit!'*[13] and lastly John in his Gospel, *'It is finished'.*[14]

Key Points to Consider:

- Matthew and Mark both record that Jesus cried out again after asking why God had forsaken him.
- None of the Gospel writers claim to provide a verbatim transcription of Jesus' utterances on the cross.
- It is not impossible that Jesus said all three things in his dying moments.

A Response:

Matthew, Mark, Luke and John are all correct. Towards the end of his suffering on the cross Jesus cried out asking why God had forsaken him (as recorded in Matthew and Mark); we are then told he cried out again. Presumably this second cry was

---

12 Mark 15:34

13 Luke 23:46

14 John 19:30

something along the lines of, 'Father, into your hands I commit my spirit. It is finished.' As is recorded in Luke and John.

The Gospel writers do not claim to tell us everything Jesus said and did. Quite the opposite, John explicitly explains that he is selectively drawing from his experiences with Jesus.[15] Each writer is telling us the truth regarding Jesus' final words, but none of them attempt to cover all of those words.

---

15 John 21:25

Who was at the Empty Tomb?

References: Matthew 28:1, Mark 16:1 and John 20:1

Type of Contradiction: Differing Accounts

The Claim: The Gospel's disagree over who was at Jesus' empty tomb on the first Easter morning.

Matthew mentions Mary Magdalene and the other Mary. Mark tells us that it was Mary Magdalene, Mary the mother of James and Salome. John only mentions Mary Magdalene.

Key Points to Consider:

- None of these accounts claim to give an exhaustive list of who was at the tomb.
- Different people may have come and gone throughout the morning.
- In Luke's gospel[16] we are told that there was a group of women (besides Mary Magdalene, Mary the mother of James and Joanna).

A Response:

It does not seem too unlikely to suppose that not all of the women came and went at precisely the same time. This is particularly true in view of them finding Jesus' body gone.

---

16 Luke 24:10

Perhaps Mary Magdalene, and some other women arrived at the tomb, found it empty, and so it was decided that she (Mary Magdalene) should wait there while the others went back to the disciples to tell them what had happened. During this time we see in John's gospel Mary has an encounter with the risen Jesus. Given the level of confusion that seems to have existed that morning, with some of Jesus' followers quick to believe he had risen from the dead, while others wondered who had stolen the body and where it had been taken; it seems entirely plausible that there would have been some coming and going to and from the tomb.

At What Time was Jesus Crucified?

References: Mark 15:25 and John 19:14

Type of Contradiction: Differing Accounts

The Claim: Mark and John contradict each other over the time of Jesus' crucifixion. Mark says it was the third hour, but John claims it was the sixth.

Key Points to Consider:

- For us 3pm is the same as 1500hrs, perhaps in a similar way Mark and John were using differing customs when describing the time.
- Mark explicitly says that Jesus was crucified at the third hour, John doesn't actually say when, merely that the trial was still going on at the sixth hour.

A Response:

The Romans counted time much as we do today, from midnight one day until midnight the next. First century Jews on the other hand regarded a day to have begun at sunset on what we would regard as the previous day. For example, Friday evening would already be Saturday, however, what they would refer to as the first hour of the day did not begin until sunrise.

If Mark was using the Jewish system then the third hour would be about 9am, if he was using the Roman system then the third hour was 3am. If John used the Jewish system then the time mentioned would be around noon, or going with the Roman system 6am. Whichever system was being used by either author the times given are not the same.

We know that Jesus was tried throughout the night, it seems then that John (using the Roman system) tells us that at 6am the trial was still in process. Mark then tells us that at 9am, the trial concludes and Jesus is sentenced to death. The times given are not the same time, however neither are the events going on at those times.

Did the Law Demand that Jesus be Executed?

References: John 18:31 and John 19:7

Type of Contradiction: Contrary Statements

The Claim: In chapter eighteen the Jewish council tells their Roman governor that it is not lawful for them to put Jesus to death. In chapter nineteen they tell that same governor that according to the law Jesus should die.

Key Points to Consider:

- They are talking about two different law codes (Jewish and Roman).

A Response:

In chapter eighteen Pilate (the Roman Governor) has become somewhat exasperated with the Jewish leaders. He doesn't really see why Jesus deserves to die, and doesn't want to be involved further. So he tells them to deal with it. They respond by saying that it was not lawful for them to put Jesus to death. That is, under Roman law they did not have the authority to carry out an execution.

In the next chapter they tell Pilate that the law demands that Jesus be put to death. This time they are speaking of their own laws, not Rome's. So, Jewish law said that Jesus (assuming his claims to divinity were not true) should be executed, Roman law demanded that this decision receive Pilate's consent.

Did Those with Paul at his Conversion Hear a Voice?

References: Acts 9:7 and Acts 22:9

Type of Contradiction: Differing Accounts

The Claim: Acts chapter nine says that those with Paul (at that time known as Saul) heard a voice at his conversion, (whilst seeing no one). Chapter twenty two says that they saw a light, and did not understand the voice. One account seems to claim they heard a voice but saw nothing; the other that they saw something but heard nothing.

Key Points to Consider:

- Chapter nine says they heard a voice, but it does not say whether or not they understood what that voice said.

- Chapter twenty two says that they saw a light, not that they saw, 'someone'.

A Response:

Any contradiction seen here is a matter of speculation, strictly speaking the two accounts found in Acts do not contradict each other. If we consider the information found in both Acts passages it seems that during Paul's conversion those who were with him saw a light, and heard a voice speaking. However, they did not see a person (that is they were not able to identify the source of the voice), nor did they understand what the voice was saying. Therefore a straight forward reading of what is contained within the book of Acts is not contradictory.

Is Justification by Faith Alone?

References: Galatians 2:16, Galatians 3:11 and James 2:21-24

Type of Contradiction: Contrary Statements

The Claim: Several times in his letter to the Galatian Christians Paul tells them that they are justified (declared righteous before God) by faith alone. James tells his readers quite the opposite, that good works are also necessary.

Key Points to Consider:

- Both James and Paul talk about faith and works, however, they use the term 'works' somewhat differently.
- Both authors were writing to address entirely different concerns and therefore have a different emphasise and different way of expressing their central point.

A Response:

I do not believe that there is any real disagreement between Paul and James. Yes they put things quite differently, but that is not the same as contradicting one another.

We must consider what both authors meant when they used terms like 'faith' and 'works':

Earlier in chapter two James illustrates what he means by 'faith alone', '*But someone will say, "You have faith and I have works." Show me your faith apart from your works, and I will show you my faith by my works. You believe that God is one; you do well. Even demons believe – and shudder.*'[17]

James' point, here and elsewhere, is that true faith in God will lead to good actions. The 'faith alone' that he speaks against is merely an intellectual acceptance of who God is, divorced from obedience, love and relationship. James says that faith in God will lead to godly living, that is to good works.

However, when Paul uses the word faith he means a commitment to a living Lord Jesus, this faith is relational, and involves obedience. For Paul, like James, true faith always goes beyond intellectual acceptance. So for both Paul and James, faith, true faith involves not only knowledge of God, but dedication and commitment to him.

The other relevant term to consider here is works, or deeds. Initially there appears to be a contradiction, James says that faith should lead to good works, Paul says that works are not necessary. However, reading both authors a little further makes it clear that they do not mean the same thing when they talk about works. For James works are godly living, things like generosity, love and obedience. Paul however, denounces the works of the law, his contention is that Jewish rituals, particularly circumcision are not needed to make a person right with God.

Paul and James are not in conflict; rather they are using terms differently and addressing different situations. Both of them agree that faith in God and righteous living are important!

---

17 James 2:18-19

Help Each Other, or Not?

References: Galatians 6:2 and Galatians 6:5

Type of Contradiction: Contrary Statements

The Claim: Within a few verses Paul is telling the Galatian Christians that they must, *'Bear one another's burdens'*[18] and that *'each will have to bear his own load'*[19]. Both can not be true!

Key Points to Consider:

- Although the words (load and burden) are similar, they are not the same, in either English or Greek.
- Both of these statements occur within a single paragraph, seemingly the author did not see them as contradictory.

A Response:

A burden could be said to be an especially heavy or difficult load. Apparently the distinction is much clearer in the original Greek, however, in the English translation it seems entirely plausible that Paul had two different sized loads in mind. He is therefore saying that there are some things in life that people can not cope with on their own, they should be helped through these times by others. However, he also wants to make it clear that in the smaller difficulties that arise day to day, each of us is primarily responsible for ourselves.

---

18 Galatians 6:2

19 Galatians 6:5

Does Every Person Sin?

References: 1st John 1:8 and 1st John 3:9

Type of Contradiction: Contrary Statements

The Claim: In 1st John 1:8 (and elsewhere in the Bible) we are told that all people do wrong things (sin). However, 1st John 3:9 seems to say the opposite, *'No one born of God makes a practise of sinning'.*[20]

Key Points to Consider:

- Strictly speaking, the statements are not actually contradictory.
- Both statements appear in a single document written by the Apostle John, it is worth asking what he meant be each of them. His purpose was presumably not to confuse!

A Response:

As with other New Testament letters 1st John was written into a specific situation. The Apostle John wrote to combat an early heresy within the church known as gnosticism. Gnostics believed that the physical world was evil, and the spiritual good. This lead some branches of gnosticism to teach that sin was not a problem, not even a reality, and righteousness not something to be sought. Rather, the goal was to escape from the evil, physical world. This was to be achieved through the acquisition of secret

---

20 1 John 3:9

knowledge, any sinful activity that seemed appealing could be indulged in.

Therefore John seeks to make it clear to his readers that all people have sinned. That is everyone has done wrong things (whether they acknowledge them or not). But also, that they, as believers should not be living lives that are characterised by sin (the gnostics where falling into both of these errors).

The two passages (1st John 1:8 and 3:9) address two separate issues. 1:8 is telling us that no one is perfect, however, 3:9 demands change and encourages Christians that their lives must not be dominated by sin.

Types of Literature

Letters

Where are they found?

Many of the New Testament books are letters: Romans, First and Second Corinthians, Galatians, Ephesians, Philippians, Colossians, First and Second Thessalonians, First and Second Timothy, Titus, Philemon, Hebrews, James, First and Second Peter, First, Second and Third John, and Jude.

Characteristics:

In many ways a New Testament letter is not so different to a twenty first century one. Letters tend to be written with a specific purpose, into a specific situation. News and advice are given, as well as greetings and other pieces of information that may be of interest to the recipient.

When we write a letter today there are certain conventions that are generally followed. For example the recipient's name is put at the beginning, the sender's at the end. Paul and the other authors of the New Testament letters wrote in accordance with the accepted style of their day.

Avoiding Potential Difficulties:

When reading a letter it will be important to consider who wrote it and, whom it was written to. Read the book from start to finish in one sitting, and take time to consider the main points made by the author as well as the reasons you believe he made them. It may also be helpful to read the introduction to a letter in a study

Bible. This will give you some extra information about the particular church that received the letter in the first place. Knowing what was going on in that church can help us to understand why the author wrote what he did.

Historical Narrative

Where is it found?

A large portion of the Bible, particularly the Old Testament (and the New Testament book of Acts) would be classified as narrative.

Characteristics:

These narratives tell the story of humanity's and Israel's history, as well as giving an account of the growth of the early church. Narratives are essentially stories, in this case true stories of God at work in history.

Avoiding Potential Difficulties:

Reading narratives we see God working to bring about his plan of redemption. We also see him partnering with human beings, who are frequently less than perfect. In reading narrative it is important to remember that we are reading about what happened, not what should have happened. Therefore, sometimes the narrative records actions, or statements that are not endorsed by the Bible as a whole. The author will not necessarily pause to say, 'such and such was incorrect'. The reader is expected to know this based on his or her understanding of what the Bible teaches elsewhere.

It is also necessary to remember that narratives are selective. That is they do not tell us everything about a particular person or event. The Apostle John explicitly states this (John 21:25), telling his readers that he has selected some (but not all) of the events he had witnessed in the life of Jesus.

If a 'contradiction' from a narrative is being discussed it will be important to consider two things. Firstly, is the narrative account giving us an example of what to do and say; or an example of what not to do and say? Secondly any 'contradiction' based on what a narrative does not say is on extremely shaky ground. Quite possibly the author omitted the event intentionally, or focused on something else which better suited his purposes.

Poetry

Where is it found?

Many books of the Bible contain at least some poetry. Of the Old Testament only Leviticus, Ruth, Esther, Haggai and Malachi have no poetry at all.

Characteristics:

Poetic writing is able to express more accurately the emotions and struggles of our hearts. This is done with the use of figurative language, words are used to paint mental pictures in the mind of the reader.

Hebrew poetry does not rely on metre or rhyme, but parallelism, which we might think of as thought rhyme. The most common type of parallelism involves two lines in which the second repeats the idea found in the first using different wording. For example:

'You have given him his heart's desire,

and have not withheld the request of his lips.'[21]

Some common literary devices found within Hebrew poetry include:

Irony – Implies something different, even the opposite of that is stated.

---

21 Psalm 21:1

Simile and Metaphor – Both are comparisons of two things that are essentially different. A simile will say that one thing is like another, a metaphor that one thing is another.

Allegory – An extended metaphor in the form of a story.

Personification – The attribution of human qualities to inanimate objects.

Hyperbole – Exaggeration with the intent of emphasis, not deception.

Anthropomorphism – The practice of describing God in human terms (physically or emotionally).

Symbols – Something stands for something else.

Avoiding Potential Difficulties:

Because of it's use of figurative language, poetic writings are frequently the source of 'contradiction'. This generally comes through an attempt to read a poetic expression of something as though it were a list of names and numbers. For example, Psalm 62:2 describes God as a rock, the reader is intended to take this figuratively as a description of God's character, firm, solid, trustworthy... we are not meant to read this and ask, 'basalt or sandstone?' That was never the author's intent and to do so misses his point completely!

The reader's goal is to discover, when and where the author has used various literary devices. To discern when a writing is intended by its author to be figurative or symbolic, as opposed to literal. These claims must be backed up by the text; that is, when a passage is to be taken figuratively that should be noticeable to anyone with an understanding of the style of writing in question. Again the reader discovers that a passage is figurative, intended to be read that way by it's author. In some cases it will be very clear, in others less so, either way approach the text with honesty and openness.

Gospels

Where are they found?

The Gospels, Matthew, Mark, Luke and John are the first four books of the New Testament.

Characteristics:

The Gospels are narratives that describe the life and death of Jesus. The word itself comes from a Greek word meaning good news.

Each gospel writer wrote with a different audience in mind; none of them sought to give a comprehensive biography of the life of Jesus. The authors are in fact highly selective, choosing material that best suits their audience.

Matthew is generally thought to have been written to the Jews. Jesus is shown to be the Messiah, the fulfilment of Old Testament prophecy.

Mark writes to encourage Roman believers during a time of persecution.

Luke writes to Gentiles, seeking to show Jesus as the saviour of sinners.

John writes to all people, with the goal that anyone who reads may come to believe in Jesus. He also shows that Jesus was both God and man.

Avoiding Potential Difficulties:

Gospel accounts do differ in details, however this is to be expected. If several people witness and report on any event, the result would be much the same. Assuming each witness tells the truth, the main points of what they observe will line up, however, in the details, each will remember something distinct. That is not contradictory, rather it paints a fuller picture.

Comparing the Gospels it must also be remembered that none of them gives a full account of Jesus' life. Each author selected stories and teachings of Jesus that suited his purpose and audience. All give us a true account of Jesus, none complete in every possible detail.

Apocalyptic Literature

Where is it found?

Most of Revelation, as well as parts of Daniel, Ezekiel and Zechariah are written in an apocalyptic style.

Characteristics:

Apocalyptic Literature was a style of writing popular amongst the Jews from about 200BC until AD 100. They express the idea that although times might currently be difficult, there will come a day when God will intervene and judge evil. This message is proclaimed using imagery and symbolism that is bizarre to modern readers, but familiar to the original audience.

The symbolism and visions are intended to convey truth, and comfort believers. They are not meant to promote fear or confusion.

Avoiding Potential Difficulties:

When reading Apocalyptic Literature keep the author's main idea before your mind. Even when you can not be sure of some of the details you should still be able to grasp the main point of the book.

Numbers often represent concepts, not statistical units. This idea is not totally foreign to us, for example, in the modern west, the number thirteen is associated with bad luck. To the ancient Jews certain numbers had similar types of meanings:

Seven stands for perfection or completion.

Three stands for God.

Four stands for the earth.

Six stands for evil (and).

Twelve for the people of God.

Because apocalypses are virtually unknown to modern readers it is necessary for us to take the time to study this type of writing before we are able to read it accurately.

Law

Where is it found?

References to the Law sometimes encompass the entire Old Testament, at other times the first five books (Genesis to Deuteronomy), or most often the body of law taking up most of Exodus chapter twenty through to the end of Deuteronomy.

Characteristics:

Broadly speaking the Law can be divided into two categories, ritual and civil laws. Ritual law concerns proper worship of God, civil law instructs the people of Israel how they should treat each other.

Avoiding Potential Difficulties:

In the Law we can see the things that God values, in particular his heart for those whom society had left vulnerable. However, it must be remembered that the Law also reflects ancient, middle eastern, patriarchal society. In a sense within the Law we see God meeting the people of ancient Israel where they were at and helping them. From their perspective the Law gave radical new rights to marginalised groups, but it was never intended as the real or final answer to human sin. Therefore, the laws of the Old Testament are not binding on Christians, unless they are re-stated in the New Testament. Nor are they intended as a blue print for an ideal modern society.

Prophecy

Where is it found?

Prophetic books make up a large part of the Old Testament. Isaiah, Jeremiah, Ezekiel, Daniel, Hosea, Joel, Amos, Obadiah, Jonah, Micah, Nahum, Habakkuk, Zephaniah, Haggai, Zechariah and Malachi are the books of the Prophets.

Characteristics:

The Prophetic books mostly consist of the words of the prophets, however, they often also contain some sections of narrative and other historical references. The central function of Old Testament prophets was to remind the people of Israel of the Law, and call them to be obedient to it. Within that role they do predict future events. It should be noted that many of the events predicted were in the prophet's future, but not in ours. The main events predicted by Old Testament prophets where the fall of Jerusalem, the fall of Samara, and the return of the Jews from Babylon. Some prophecies (although only a small percentage) predict the coming of Jesus, the church age, and final judgement.

Avoiding Potential Difficulties:

To understand the prophets a knowledge of their situation is important. For many of their words to make sense we must know what was happening in the nation of Israel at the time they spoke. Reading the relevant parts of Kings, and study Bible notes can help supply us with this information.

Most prophecies are written in a poetic form, using language that is full of symbolism and different figures of speech. Therefore some familiarity with Hebrew poetry will assist us in reading the prophets with understanding.

Wisdom

Where is it found?

Job, Proverbs, Ecclesiastes and Song of Songs are considered the wisdom books of the Old Testament. However, wisdom literature is also found in some parts of the Psalms, Habakkuk and James.

Characteristics:

Wisdom literature was common in the ancient world. The goal was to pass on what people had learnt through their own life experiences. Wisdom writings are meant to be intensely practical, Biblical wisdom assumes a knowledge of God and his ways, and it is meant to be lived out, not debated.

Avoiding Potential Difficulties:

Proverbs gives the reader concise, practical sayings for successful everyday life. These statements are often worded to be memorable, not technically precise; and it must be remembered that they are statements of general truth, not promises.

The wisdom of Job and Ecclesiastes looks at some of the hard issues of life. Why do bad things happen to good people? And what is the meaning of life? With these it is particularly important to read the entire book! Both Job and Ecclesiastes take us on a journey, different thoughts are looked at and rejected along the way; therefore reading verses in isolation may lead to a misunderstanding of the authors' main point.

www.ingramcontent.com/pod-product-compliance
Ingram Content Group UK Ltd.
Pitfield, Milton Keynes, MK11 3LW, UK
UKHW041929190726
13854UKWH00004B/1518

9 781257 771349